COME INTO MY PARLOUR

Come into my parlour

CAUTIONARY VERSES AND INSTRUCTIVE TALES FOR THE NEW MILLENNIUM

Bill Richardson

illustrated by Chum McLeod

POLESTAR
BOOK PUBLISHERS

Published by:
Polestar Press Ltd.
1011 Commercial Drive, Second Floor
Vancouver, BC
V5L 3X1

The Publisher would like to acknowledge the financial assistance of
The Canada Council, British Columbia Cultural Services Branch,
and the Department of Canadian Heritage.

Cover art by Chum McLeod
Cover design by Chum McLeod and Sandra Robinson
Author photo by Daniel Collins
Production by Michelle Benjamin
Printed in Canada by Best-Gagne

Canadian Cataloguing in Publication Data

Richardson, Bill,
        Come into my parlour
ISBN 0-919591-85-X
 1. Humorous poetry, Canadian (English)* 2. Limericks. I. Title.
PS8585.I186C6 1994   C811'.54   C94-910125-7
PR9199.3R52C6 1994

To Margaret Meikle, Beloved Know-It-All

Come Into My Parlour

"Yet another great truth I record in my verse…"
   — Hilaire Belloc
    "The Viper"

"Serve up in a clean dish, and throw the whole out of the window as fast as possible."
   — Edward Lear
    "To Make an Amblongus Pie"

Introduction
by Romana Clay, R.N.

COME INTO MY PARLOUR IS BILL RICHARDSON'S second collection of verse, and it contains what is surely his finest work to date. Readers who believed The Bard had attained the very apogee of poetical possibility with the morsels contained in his last volume will find themselves slack-jawed with wonder to see him surpass himself herein, again and again.

In the nearly two years that have elapsed since the publication of *Queen Of All The Dustballs*, I have had the singular privilege of maintaining close, indeed almost daily, contact with Mr. Richardson, the self-appointed Poet Laureate of Canada. I have gained this access to so notoriously retiring an individual because, through a set of circumstances too complex to go into here*, I have become both his nurse, and his conduit to the Muse. Blessed am I among women!

My present situation is rather akin to that of a wildlife biologist who conceals herself in a chill and constricting blind in order to observe the habits, both diurnal and nocturnal, of some rare and endangered species. This is an apt metaphor. For make no mistake: this is a society that embraces neither poetry nor the poor possessed creatures who create it. That Mr. Richardson has maintained a cheerful mien while dodging the many brickbats that have been tossed his way is astonishing. That he has scaled ever hoarier summits of excellence while so assailed is more astonishing still.

---

*see *Queen of All The Dustballs*, pp. 9-15.

How I wish I could convey to you the wonder of it all! I have watched him take rude and rough-hewn quotidian experience; watched him go after it with the belt sander of his Art; watched him grind it down and grind it down and grind it down some more, until the loveliest of grains is revealed in all its splendour. I have seen him take the most unlikely of nuggets, fire it in the refining furnace of his sensibilities, and bring forth into the world a ring of the purest gold. All this he does with only occasional injections of opiates. Rarely do I hear him cry, "Praise the Lord and pass the Prozac!" And when he does, I know he is hot on the trail of something really, really good.

Mr. Richardson is painfully shy and rarely grants interviews, in spite of constant hounding by the international media. He accorded me the honour of a short Question and Answer session some months ago, as he was preparing *Come Into My Parlour* for publication. The interview was published in the quarterly, *Fairly Vain: Views From The Moral High Ground*. It is reprinted here by permission of the editors, in the hope that it will give Mr. Richardson's readers deeper insight into his *oeuvre*. Our conversation took place in the salon of Casa Sordida, Mr. Richardson's small and, it must be said, somewhat shabby, flat in downtown Vancouver. That so gifted an artist should be compelled to endure such down-at-the-heel circumstances is a telling indictment of how undervalued poets are in Canada, his home and native land.

RC: *Come Into My Parlour* is a collection of cautionary tales. I should say they owe their inspiration to the work of Hilaire Belloc, who wrote two volumes of mock didactic poems, ostensibly for children. Such poems, dealing with questions of manners and overall deportment, were, I need scarcely note, part of the baggage of the Victorian nursery. Would you concur?

BR: Sure.

RC: So would you say then, that these are gentle jeremiads, which underscore in a loving but nevertheless telling way, the foibles and peccadilloes to which we are all heir because we are, after all, human and fallible? And that you have laid special emphasis on those oddities that are so much a part and parcel of living in these dangerous end years of the century? A phrase which you yourself have used on more occasions than I can count?

BR: Yeah, I guess.

RC: You have fulfilled the function of self-appointed Poet Laureate of Canada for over six years, now. And still, a recent survey demonstrates that less than .02% of the population knows who the hell you are! In fact, in name recognition tests, you scored even lower than the inventor of margarine!

BR: Who was that, Nurse Clay?

RC: I've forgotten. The point is, most artists would have recognized they were fighting a losing battle; that they were fulfilling an imagined need that had no basis in anything remotely resembling reality. Most artists would have given up the struggle, thrown in the towel, gone on to seek out greener pastures. And yet, you persist in writing your verses, one after the other! Why, surely you recognize that no one would care or notice if you never wrote another word, or if you fell off the face of the earth tomorrow. Would you care to comment?

BR: Do you mind if I smoke?

RC: Yes. I wonder if you'd care to comment, Mr. Richardson, on your *modus operandi* for the writing of poetry? Such things are of little interest to the public at large, but students sometimes want to know. I have observed that your principal motivators are that special panic that comes of having nothing on a page two hours before a deadline; and an unseemly dollop of single malt scotch. Is this, perhaps, the source of the numerous factual slip-ups in your *oeuvre*, as well as the many shortcomings that mar both your diction and scansion?

BR: I'd never thought of it before. Maybe you're right.

RC: Your critics, whose number is legion, suggest that you are not a poet at all, but simply a hanger-on to the lifeboat of Art, an ersatz versifier with a freakish gift for shamelessness, an *idiot pas très savant* who can't think of any other way to make a living. How would you answer these charges?

BR: Care for a scotch, Nurse Clay?

RC: Thank you. And finally, do you have any words of advice for young poets who might stumble on this book in a remainder bin or at the Hadassah Bazaar — advice on how best to avoid the pitfalls and potholes that have so perilously littered the road you have followed, never flagging, to your present state of unalloyed mediocrity?

BR: On the rocks, Nurse Clay? Or straight up?

RC: On the rocks. Thank you, Mr. Richardson. Thank you for your time. Thank you for your work. Thank you for being you.

And so, dear reader, you are now primed for the selection of instructive verses which follows. Mr. Richardson assures me that his prime motivation in writing these little cautionary tales has been, first and foremost, the betterment of us all. The Bard would like to thank those listeners to CBC Radio whose stories inspired some of these tales. He would also like to thank his colleagues there, most particularly Rosemary Allenbach and Vicki Gabereau. Thanks abounding, too, to Michelle Benjamin, Julian Ross, and Chum McLeod. Come along, then! Come into his parlour and behold the wonders that await you there.

Romana Clay, R.N.
Casa Sordida
April, 1994

onsider all the strangenesses that in the world abide...

My Handbag and I

Here, Mr. Richardson tackles one of western civilization's Great Imponderables: what exactly does the Queen carry in her purse? This is one of The Poet's most insightful studies, and he hopes its warning against excessive curiosity will be taken to heart by the paparazzi who plague his days, and dog his every step.

Consider all the strangenesses that in the world abide:
The secrets of the pyramids, the workings of the tides,
The way the salmon struggles home before it deigns to spawn,
The way that moles infest your own and not your neighbour's lawn.
These puzzles and conundrums might befuddle and confuse,
But nothing's so dumbfounding, so with mystery suffused,
So likely to be-line a brow and common sense disperse
As trying to discern what lurks within the monarch's purse.

What's in the good Queen's handbag? We all wonder what she stows.
It can't be kleenex as she never needs to blow her nose.
Encumbrances that might belong to any one of us —
Like quarters for the telephone, or tokens for the bus,
Or stubs from sundry tickets, or a stray, discarded mint
Gone sticky from the heat and all bespecked with bits of lint,
Or bills she's yet to pay, or shades of lipstick to apply,
Or recipes she's clipped and swears she's one day going to try,

Or possibly a rabbit's foot she hopes will bring her luck,
Or photos of the kiddies: Eddie, Andy, Annie, Chuck —
No, none of these pedestrian accoutrements are found
Within the handbag that she never sets upon the ground.
And this point is germane to us. Which one of us has spied
The Queen without some kind of clutch she clutches to her side?
No, not in recent memory. When queens take to the streets
They've got a handbag that they'll not relinquish or release.

And that's because of Tom, the lad who lived up to his name,
Who peeped inside the handbag and was nevermore the same.
It was years ago, near Brandon, and the Queen was passing through,
Traipsing 'round the realm the way that queens are wont to do.
She met some local seniors, and she paid the Mayor a call,
Performing every task with all regard for protocol,
She took the fragrant flowers, and she smiled at every band,
And never did the bag she carried leave her white-gloved hand.

Tommy's parents' farm had been included on her tour.
They were famous in the region for their tried and true manure.
And it was said their corgis were a sight that must be seen
Especially by a monarch who's a corgi-loving queen.
It happened there were puppies who were romping in the barn.
The Queen surveyed their frolics and was more than slightly charmed.
So she could better pick one up and hold it in her palm,
She turned and gave her handbag to — I hate to say it — Tom.

Now, Tom was only seven, so he really can't be blamed.
He could not know that he was doomed to never be the same.
Before someone could stop him he had grasped the clasp and pried
The purse so it was open and then Tommy looked inside.
He must have seen what it contained, perceived its secret loot.
But at that very moment little Tommy was struck mute.
The final sound he uttered was an awful, piercing shriek.
"What's wrong young Tom?" his mother cried, but Tommy could not speak.

They stuck his head between his knees, they whacked him on the back,
The Queen discreetly scooped and closed her violated sack.
"I hope that he gets better soon," she said, "we have to go.
Toodle-oo! I'm sure your dogs will win the best of show!"
She took her fawning retinue. They hailed the limousine.
She took her purse and in it all that little Tom had seen.
The lad, alas, did not improve. He entered catatonia,
And there remained, as active as your typical begonia.

Whatever had he seen therein that made him quail and fail?
The Lost Ark of the Covenant? Or else, the Holy Grail?
Some ancient, potent totem from some lost, forgotten land,
The sight of which initiates alone can bear to stand?
Some strange hermetic heraldry, a dark Masonic ring,
Or else the Shroud of Buckingham, or some such other thing?
It really doesn't matter. I've fulfilled my chosen task.
What's inside the monarch's purse? It's better not to ask.

bunch of the boys were whooping it up...

Service Is Rendered

Perhaps it was inevitable that some fool would one day challenge Mr. Richardson's claim to self-appointed Poet Laureateship. A gentleman — let's give him the benefit of the doubt — who was also named Bill, sent The Poet an extremely rude and presumptuous note in which he advanced his own claim on the position Mr. Richardson occupies by simple dint of the fact he created it. The Incumbent dashed off the following response in the merest of minutes, and the Pretender, properly cowed by so virtuosic a display, was never heard from again. The moral is: if you want to play with the big guns, bring along some ammo. The Bard was weaned on the poetry of Robert Service, and this poem is a salute to that great chronicler of the glory days of the gold rush.

A bunch of the boys were whooping it up, the salon was thick with talk,
The kid that handled the music box was tinkling inventions by Bach.
Back of the bar in a sonnet game sat bilious, limpid Bill.
And watching him scrawl, as she leaned 'gainst the wall, was the lady that's
    known as Lil.

That Lil loved Bill could be distilled by the heaves of her mountainous chest.
She furrowed her brow as she watched him now on his dauntless poetical
    quest:
Before he died he had vowed to try to discover a rhyme for "orange,"
But write though he might, from the morning till night, the best he could
    manage was "door hinge."

Then out of the night that was tepid and dank and into the hum of the words,
There stumbled a fellow whose mien and demeanour betrayed him as kind of
a nerd,
His glasses were smudged and his laces were fudged and you knew he had ring
'round the collar.
The kid at the keyboard had taken a break. He sat down and thumped out
some Mahler.

There's men that somehow just hold your eyes and make your knees trembly
and weak,
And such was he though a fool could see he was plainly a bit of a geek.
But God! When he played the whole place swayed and shook with a shudder-
ing chill:
But chill turned to freeze when he slammed down the keys and yelled, "Show
me the poet called Bill!"

The room fell dead and a cry full of dread was welling in all of their craws,
Then up Bill rose, struck a machismo pose, and sneeringly answered "*C'est
moi*."
The new rude dude, big on attitude, told him, "Fella, you're outta your prime:
For I'm called Bill too, and I've news for you. It's *me* who's the guru of
rhyme."

The lady called Lil looked from Bill back to Bill and emitted a tremulous
   wheeze:
Tension brought on an asthmatic condition: she'd cough and she'd splutter
   and sneeze.
She trembled, turned paler, she took her inhaler, and over a thudding
   "Achoo!"
She heard her man Bill say to Bill the pretender: "So you're the new guru. Says
   who?"

"Says me and my grandma," the newcomer stammered in tones that no
   goodwill would foster.
"Your time here is through for I've slyly construed you're a charlatan, fake and
   imposter,
Your raving, polemical poems alchemical don't mean a jot or a tittle!
For you can't rhyme orange, but as sure as I'm born, the word that you're
   seeking is ——————— !"

The room held its breath, Bill and Lil clutched their breasts (that is, clutched
   their own — not each others' —
It's a family tome and my research has shown that a randy poem generates
   bother.)
All at once in the room, there was smoke, flame and fume, and the floor-
   boards were splintered asunder,
A hand straight from hell grabbed the know-it-all Bill and pulled him protest-
   ing down under.

The truth is forlorn, but the fact is that orange's rhyme is known just to the
    devil,

I know it's far-fetched after all this kvetch, but I swear that I'm straight on the
    level.

The sulfur smell's gone from the stylish salon where Bill can't do better than
    orange;

The rhyme can't be found, not by Auden or Pound. An orange is orange is
    orange.

And They Were Snore Afraid

The Poet has, from time to very occasional time, found himself in the horizontal position beside individuals with acute cases of sleep apnea. None of those so afflicted could be convinced that they snored. This tale, which also owes its inspiration to Robert Service, most particularly "The Cremation of Sam McGee," warns against the peculiar vanity that prevents so many people from seeking the professional help that will allow them to stop being pests and become worthwhile, productive members of society.

Come, children! Gather 'round me then, and hear my exhortation!
This sickly string of syllables, this windy postulation
Will tell the tale of Christopher, a tale both sad and moving,
A tale which, if you lend an ear, you'll surely find improving.

From the day that Christopher was just a lad in britches —
Scaling trees and scooping frogs and pollywogs from ditches —
Just when healing slumber from its pitcher started pouring,
He would open wide his jaws and give himself to snoring.

And we are not just talking, friends, about a little grumble,
A gentle snort or grunt or two as through his dreams he tumbled.
Oh, no! Sweet little Christopher was rather the inflictor
Of seismic rumblings that could tip the scale devised by Richter.

ome, children! Gather 'round
me then...

Oh, yes! Sweet little Christopher, before the age of seven,
Directly his devotions had been ferried off to Heaven
And well before the angels had completed their collation,
Would shake the roof and chimney top and challenge the foundation.

Now, when his several siblings and his parents and the neighbours
Tried to ascertain just why his breathing grew so laboured,
Suggesting that perhaps they might seek out some sage physician,
Christopher grew truculent and took this firm position:

"I don't know what you're on about!" he'd answer their entreating,
"I'm sure I never snore," he'd say, rejecting such a meeting.
They made their testimonials, and tapes, too, that they played him
But nothing they could say or do was able to persuade him.

He'd say, "Why, that's a backhoe, or a garbage truck unloading,
Or possibly a potent bomb recorded while exploding,
Or tanks and mortars raging in a pitched and awful battle.
But no one built of flesh could make that phlegmy, awful rattle."

So, Christopher summarily rejected all their counsel.
Every night a wheezing ululation wracked his tonsils,
Every night his family was, in larger measure, deafened.
Time went by and finally they packed their bags and left him.

Ever was it thus. Chris left a trail both wide and gory.
At college he was driven from a dozen dormitories,
And every time he married — and he went through many spouses —
They never stood a chance unless they lived in separate houses.

Time went by and Christopher was ostracized and censured,
Time went by, his hair grew grey, his teeth gave way to dentures.
But Chris could never see the truth, nor come to the admission,
That snoring such as he produced might just as well be fission.

Eventually his body from his wretched soul was fractured:
I mean to say our hero died, flew on to greener pastures.
No one came to claim him, nor wrote poems in memoriam.
Christopher was taken to the local crematorium.

The keeper of the furnaces took on his new assignment,
He rolled his sleeves and primed the fires for Chris's quick consignment.
The hellish doors were opened, he was ready to deliver
When all at once he heard a noise that made him halt and shiver.

Yes — shiver in the face of flames, and set aside his bellows.
A sound like "GRRNAAXXIIAAAEEEYOWWSHHH" alarmed the worthy fellow.
It came from in the casket! Such events don't happen often;
Quickly then he pried the lid from off the oaken coffin.

"Hey Bud!" the shocked cremation man exclaimed. Chris raised his noggin.
"Wake up! Wake up! You almost hit the flames in this toboggan!
Wake up! Wake up! You're snoring!" Chris sat up with flaring nostrils.
"Snoring? Go to Hell!" he roared, astonishingly hostile.

"Oh yeah?" replied the stoker, as he pulled the fateful lever:
Christopher slid on and his connection here was severed.
These then are the words he spoke as he passed into Hades:
"I do not snore! I've never snored! No buts! No ifs! No maybes!"

What then is the lesson of this cautionary epic?
The salve that is contained herein, the moral antiseptic
Is simply that a strong belief, impervious to suasion,
Can sometimes land its owner in the damnest situations.

There's a seaside town known as
Southampton —

In Wadsworth Country

Mr. Richardson, as has been demonstrated in the last two selections, is not impervious to influence. When he feels that a debt is owed, but cannot recollect the source, he undergoes a session of hypnotherapy so that he might give credit where credit is due. It was in such an altered state that he confessed this poem owes a great deal, rhythmically, to "Albert and the Lion," that Stanley Holloway music hall number. The poem was written at the request of Dave. Along with his wife Vivienne, Dave went back to his home town of Southampton, to visit relatives. He imbibed too much of the local ale, and found himself, shortly thereafter, starkers on the High Road. This was the bare outline on which The Bard based one of his naughtier verses.

There's a seaside town known as Southampton —
In England, remote from these shores.
Dave went there to have his vacation:
No matter he'd been there before!
He took his beloved wife Vivienne
To visit their daughter Lorraine:
Though Vivienne told all her cronies
She'd rather have travelled to Spain.

"I can fairly predict what will happen,"
She told her Canadian friends:
"My Davey will go on a bender,
And Heaven knows how it will end.
He'll start to get rather nostalgic,
Then knock back a Guinness or six,
And it won't be too long, you can wager
Before he'll be up to his tricks.

"For Dave, when he has a pint in him,
Has sometimes been known to try
To get all conciliatory,
And telephone Charles and Di.
It happens each time that we visit.
I haven't the faintest of doubts
He'll try to go straight to the monarch
And offer to straighten things out."

Now, Vivienne's words were prophetic.
They went out one night with some chums
And Dave started guzzling Wadsworth:
"Can't get this where I've just come from!"
He said as he ordered another,
A pint that he hastily downed.
"Again for the road, good bartender,"
He called to command one more round.

When finally last call was sounded —
"Time gentlemen, please, to be gone," —
Dave ordered and knocked back another
While Vivienne went to the john.
They headed back home to their daughter's.
She lived on the Priory Road.
Dave ducked once or twice into alleys,
The better to lighten his load.

Long-suffering Vivienne waited,
And said, "Come on, don't take all night!"
She told him, "You know you're disgusting!"
Dave smirked and he answered, "You're right."
There's a curious thing about liquor:
When someone gets pissed to the gills
He loses his access to memory:
It gets washed away with the swill.

He tends to forego recollection
If he is sufficiently drunk,
And such was the case with our hero:
Dear Davey was totally skunked.
Though not prone to somnambulation,
He nonetheless rose from his cot
And went for a scenic meander,
Displaying what nature had wrought.

He cannot say just how it happened,
He only knows when he came to
That he was *al fresco*, and walking —
Though no longer wearing his shoes.
His footwear he'd somehow discarded,
His shirt too had gone by the way,
His undies had left without waving:
He stood there in some disarray.

He stood there all starkers and nekkid,
In total contempt of the law.
He cast down his eyes, all contented,
And rather enjoyed what he saw.
"Hello there, my friend," Davey muttered,
And whistled with nary a care
A tune about lovely coconuts:
Bunches, or maybe a pair.

Had constables stumbled upon him
All puckered and whistling with zeal,
They'd surely arrest him, well-knowing
He hadn't a weapon concealed.
But God, who looks out for the simple,
Took pity on poor Davey's plight.
He sent down a sobering angel
To guide him back home through the night.

He took the poor sod by the elbow —
For Davey was starting to wilt —
And no one on Priory witnessed
The wares that he hides 'neath his kilt.
Unseen by police or by neighbours,
And winked at by stars overhead,
The angel took Dave to his daughter's
And tucked him all safely in bed.

He cuddled up next to his Vivienne,
And whispered "Old Viv! Good as gold!"
"You're plastered," she cooed to her husband,
"And what's more, my darling, you're cold!"
Praise God that He suffers fools gladly,
Praise Heaven he sees that they're saved.
Ulysses returns to the homestead:
And that ends the saga of Dave.

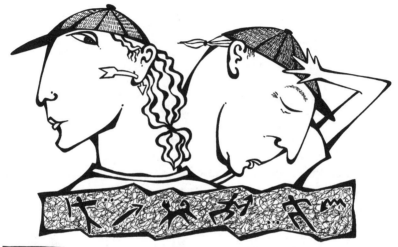

emory's a mystery. We wonder
where it dwells.

An Ear Piercing Cry

In years gone by, the piercing of ears was a rite of passage young women went through, often in the company of their mothers. Latterly, young men have been undergoing this minor surgery, and many fathers go along for the ride. A surprising number of papas have themselves willingly offered up their lobes for this ritual mutilation. The Poet is skeptical. He looks askance on men in their forties who foolishly cling to the things of youth, and here issues a warning against fathers following fashion trends that properly belong to their sons.

Memory's a mystery. We wonder where it dwells.
In the corrugated brain, or locked in every cell?
And can we only recollect our own dull, daily grind?
Or do we access, on occasion, some collective mind?

I rather think the latter for, from time to time, it seems
A world that's surely not my own emerges from my dreams:
A world that's leagues removed from mine: Remote. Exotic. New.
So foreign, yet familiar somehow. Classic *déjà-vu!*

Some ancient tribal recollection rises to the fore,
And I see things that touch me, stir me, to my very core.
I see a father teach his son to wield a deadly spear,
To creep through tangled underbrush, to tell when game is near,

To heave the lance, to pierce the heart, to take the meat and hide.
And when, reluctantly, I wake, when from that place I'm pried,
It seems so real! I can but think that somehow I have tapped
The trunk of common memory, and siphoned off the sap.

And twenty generations hence, when someone like me sleeps —
The tea of antique memory is brewed, and strong and steeped —
He'll kickstart his subconscious, and start revving up *les rêves*:
What will be the potent dreams that future mind will have?

Will he wake with wonderment, or with a sense of awe,
And later at the office tell his colleagues what he saw?:
"I saw a man in middle age and with him was a lad:
The younger was called Jason, and the older was called Dad.

"They both were swathed in denim, and a totem of their tribe
Were caps that bore the logo 'Bluejays' lovingly inscribed.
Each one had a ponytail, though Dad had thinning locks,
And on their feet were army boots that Jason labelled 'Docs.'

"They strode inside a jewelery store. Said Dad, all gruff and fierce:
'The boy and me are here because we want our earlobes pierced.'
A woman with important hair retrieved the piercing tool.
Little Jason sat astride her sacrificial stool.

"He pointed to the left lobe, and she clutched the flap of skin,
Struck with serpent quickness and behold! The stud was in!
And oh, but he was brave! He never screamed or even squirmed.
'Cool!' was all he said, and then to Dad — 'Okay, your turn.'

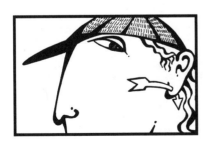

"Dad was watching carefully. He saw his son impaled.
His brow had turned all sweaty and his face had gone all pale.
His breath was coming rapidly. He had a worried look.
And as he sat astride the stool he trembled and he shook.

"'Left or right?' the priestess asked. Before poor dad could say
He gagged and then he gurgled and he fainted dead away.
Jason sighed the sigh of one who badly suffers fools.
'Dad,' he groaned. The grown man moaned. 'That's just so, so uncool!'"

Twenty generations hence, when someone tells this dream,
His listeners will scratch their heads, and wonder what it means.
Perhaps someone who's heard of Jung, or studied him at college,
Will mutter something vague about the source of common knowledge,

Of ancient rites of passages, of primitives and magic.
If this is all we leave behind, methinks it's rather tragic.
Worshipers of fashion take a calculated gamble,
Risking the construing of some future Joseph Campbell.

What will archaeologists who excavate the psyche
Make of our reliance on Adidas, Docs and Nikes?
Who will clean the wellspring up? Who dares to dig that deep?
Not me, babe. I'm going to kick my Nikes off and sleep.

 see the sure and certain signs...

About Facials

Late nights, smoky cafés, worries about money, the rigours of the creative life: all these have taken their toll on The Poet's skin. He is fond of the occasional facial, and is not ashamed to admit it. Here, however, he describes what happened to him the day he was lounging about, wearing nothing but a mask of mud, when a fire alarm sounded, compelling him to scamper out of his building and into the busy street below. Vanity has its price, and its price is sometimes high.

I see the sure and certain signs
My face is done for, now.
The skin is wrinkled round my eyes,
The furrows on my brow
Look as though I fell beneath
A glacier or a plough.

And though I sleep eight hours each night
I'm told that I look tired.
So in the slough of slow decay
I'm well and truly mired.
It's plain that plastic surgery
Will one day be required.

It's not quite at that point just yet,
And even though I brood
I know that for the moment
I need just an oil and lube.
And so I buy a facial masque
That squeezes from a tube.

I've tried out several different brands
Designed for dermal duds.
Avocado, aloe vera,
Mint and oatmeal mud.
Each, when smeared, looks rather like
The crud left by a flood.

I spread it on capaciously
Around my eyes and cheeks,
I lay a thick, substantial layer
Along my chin and beak,
Then simply lie to let it dry:
This happens once a week.

I rest for twenty minutes, then,
Grotesque, besmeared, a fright.
But oh, I love the way it pulls
The skin and makes it tight!
And what is more it seals the pores.
I used one just last night.

Imagine me upon the couch:
All naked, slightly curled
Around the dog and purring cat
My face with oatmeal burled.
I sipped a glass of single malt
And watched "The Golden Girls."

A meditative state of mind
Pervaded overall.
I felt a sense of ease and calm,
Removed from psychic squalls.
How glad I was to have again
A facial overhaul.

Each flower needs a bud to bloom,
Each bud must have its worm.
When someone pulled the fire alarm
This theory was confirmed.
My pure unalloyed happiness
Fast reached its end of term.

I acted with the swift response
Of one both lithe and spry,
My reflex hastened on because
I'm disinclined to fry.
I caged the cat and leashed the dog
And towelled my loins and thighs.

A towel about my midriff
And my chest and tootsies bare,
We followed regulations
And we hurried down the stairs,
We exited the fire door
And strode out in the air.

You ought to know I'm not among
The muscular elect.
It's not the kind of body
One would linger to inspect.
I fear that I'd neglected to
Consider the effect.

Picture, if you will, the scene:
My building is downtown.
The street outside is busy,
Cars and passers-by abound.
I stand there with a dog and cat,
Swathed in my ersatz gown.

It's short and made of terrycloth,
Madonna, say, or Prince
Could bring off such a garment.
Not a single soul would wince.
But I was ill-advised
To thus bedecked step out to mince.

"Perhaps he's on a day pass,"
Said a husband to his wife,
"He looks to me like one they should
Have locked away for life."
"His face!" she said, "I only hope
He hasn't got a knife."

My neighbours, who had come out too,
Took one look and recoiled
To see my odd and scant attire,
To see my visage soiled.
Suffice it just to say my day
Was absolutely spoiled.

Clad like an errant bushman
Who had just misplaced his spear,
I tried for tribal dignity
While holding back my tears.
The firemen came and smelled no smoke,
Declared the coast was clear.

I dragged the dog and hiked the cat
Upstairs to my abode,
Doffed my towel and set aside
My burdens and my load.
I stood before the mirror,
My face configured like a toad.

I wiped away the mask. *Voila!*
My wrinkles were all gone.
Toad no more, but now a prince,
Not pale and wan or drawn.
Too bad my friends can't see me —
I'm in hiding from now on.

I'd kept my wicker rocking chair
for nigh on fifteen years...

Generous, To A Fault

The Poet's veins gush with the milk of human kindness. He bestowed a beloved rocking chair on the son of a friend. The young man was setting up his first apartment. Unfortunately, The Poet neglected to take into account that this was his cat's favourite perch. She whined loudly for some weeks after it was taken away. This is a fanciful account of her attempts to retrieve her cherished bit of wicker.

I'd kept my wicker rocking chair for nigh on fifteen years:
I'd had it in a dozen small apartments.
It bore its silent witness to the laughter and the tears
That ricochet throughout the heart's compartments.

The loving and the leaving, the beginnings and the ends,
The fretting and forgetting and forgiving,
The transient acquaintances, the plenitude of friends,
The small defeats and triumphs we call living.

I bought that chair for 40 bucks when I was twenty-three:
Those days before the advent of recession.
Now in my middle years I find I'm longing to be free
Of cumbersome, material possessions.

I'm entering some Buddhist phase, and so the other day,
I said, "I own this chair, and though I've loved it
My spirit will be burnished if I give the thing away."
A friend's young son came by, and he removed it.

It didn't hurt to see it go. It happened in a flash,
Without the need to haggle or to dicker.
This wasn't a transaction that exacted any cash.
I'd made a willing present of the wicker.

My heart was full of happiness. My soul was full of light.
My being was completely incandescent.
I'd freed myself of longing, seen that earthly things are trite,
And given something cherished as a present.

My cat is not a Buddhist, though, and she was less than thrilled.
She thought my generosity a blunder.
She cast a baleful look at me — a look which, if looks killed,
Would have me writing this from six feet under.

"I liked that chair, you bastard," she intoned in tongue of cat.
"How dare you let it exit my dominion!
It won't be gone for long, however, I can promise that!
I've got my wiles, and what's more — I have minions!"

She waited till I fell asleep. She heard me snore and wheeze,
And then she rifled through my every pocket.
She said a soft "Eureka" when she finally found my keys,
She tiptoed to the door, and then unlocked it.

Before she left, she woke the dog. The night was full of stars,
A night designed for baying and for barking.
"Quiet, bitch," the cat intoned, "and get into the car.
You're going to drive." They left the covered parking.

The dog was at the wheel, the cunning cat was at her side,
Two miscreants, intent on dirty duty.
Like Thelma and Louise they felt that swelling felon's pride —
Their minds were bent on bringing home the booty.

Their minds were bent on capturing the chair that got away,
They'd wrest it from the grasp of the pretender
Who thought he owned the throne, but who, if these two had their way,
Would mark the thing, "Return, *tout de suite*, to sender."

Alas, they passed a hydrant, and the doggy-on-a-spree
Proved herself unable to ignore it.
"Excuse me for a second, while I take a break and pee,"
She said, and steered the speeding car toward it.

She hadn't got the brakes quite right. I guess that she misjudged,
Nor was the cat her canniest advisor.
The long and short is that, somehow, the heist was finally fudged,
When they produced a gushing urban geyser.

The cops of course were summoned, and they brought the truants home,
And heaped on me their stern disapprobation.
They said a proper parent wouldn't let his children roam,
I ought to be in jail, or on probation.

"Can someone please explain," I said, when they had finally gone,
"Why you had to put me through these rigours?"
The cat sat where the chair had been and looked out at the dawn,
And yawned and blinked and muttered, "*Purr.* Go figure."

I'll go out then tomorrow and I'll buy another chair,
Just like the one with which the cat is smitten.
The next time I feel Buddhist, feel the need to thin and pare,
I'll give away the puppy and the kitten.

Katy had a kitty and the kitty's name
was Jezebel...

Independent Claws

This poem requires little introduction. It need only be noted that Mr. Richardson was intrigued to see how cat scratching posts seem designed with ugliness first and foremost in mind, and that cats are very disinclined to use them. This is his speculative and cautionary analysis of why this might be so.

Katy had a kitty and the kitty's name was Jezebel,
Katy's kitty Jezzy was a beauty free of flaws,
Save the fact that Jezzy, cuddly cutie, funny fuzzy ball
Came equipped with attitude and sharp and nasty claws.

Katy had a sofa, very stylish, plush and comfortable,
Katy had a sofa that could double as a bed,
Katy's kitty Jezzy thought the sofa bed was wonderful,
Grand to jump and gambol on, and tons of fun to shred.

Jezzy sunk her talons in the velveteen upholstery,
Raked them port to starboard, nave to chops and stem to stern,
Katy was depressed to watch the progress of its mouldering.
"Jezzy," she'd admonish, "will you never, ever learn?"

Katy finally thought to stall these inclinations criminal,
Bring about reform before her chesterfield was toast.
"Should I try the obvious," she thought, "or go subliminal?"
Katy chose the former, and acquired a scratching post.

Oh, but it was nasty! It was more than slightly hideous:
Six feet tall and carpeted with shag in orangey tones.
Katy gagged to see it, but her kitty's ways invidious
Warranted its purchase, so she paid and dragged it home.

"Kitty, kitty, kitty," she exclaimed as she was entering,
"Jezzy, Jezzy, Jezebel," she trilled as she installed
In her stylish living room the post, to end the rendering
Of her lovely sofa once and finally for all.

Jezebel was napping and was wakened by this blustering,
Jezzy rose and preened and stretched, like any other cat.
Katy waited by the post, within her heart hope mustering:
Jezzy took one look and wondered, "What the hell is that?"

"Jezzy has a prezzy!" cooed the hopeful human, sappily.
"Look! A pretty scratching post! No need for more rebukes!
Now you needn't claw the couch, and we can both live happily!"
"Clear the room," thought Jezzy, "'cause I think I'm gonna puke!"

Jezebel was unimpressed. She turned her back and naughtily
Jumped up on the sofa and embedded there her nails.
Katy scratched the scratching post to show her how, but haughtily
Jezebel displayed disdain by lifting up her tail.

Jezebel displayed disdain by showing her posterior
While the sound of ripping fabric rippled through the room.
Katy did her level best to keep a cool exterior
While her inner landscape was awash with doom and gloom.

Sachets filled with catnip were attached to the extremities
Of the shaggy scratching post that merited such scorn.
Nothing Katy did, alas, could whittle down the enmity
'Twixt the cat and hated post: so, Kate gave up, forlorn.

Nothing could convince the cat to use that shaggy implement.
Jezebel was adamant: she far preferred to rip
Fabric from the sofa, in accruing velvet increments;
Katy's ministrations simply gave the puss the pip.

Who among us can explain the kitten's firm perversity?
Why did she abhor the post, and like the couch a lot?
No one needs advanced degrees from fancy universities
Just to see the post was ugly, and the couch was not.

Bear, therefore, all this in mind, ye with *felis domesticus*:
If you wish your furniture to linger long intact,
Buy attractive scratching posts, but ugly chairs are best because
Absence of aesthetics is repellent to a cat.

The story of Bartimaeus…

Bartimaeus

The Arnolds of Riondel, B.C. told Mr. Richardson about their goat, Bartimaeus, whose blindness does not prevent him from having a good time. Note that The Poet abandons the strict rhyme scheme he favours for something a little more Stevie Smith. The High Anglican tone of the piece seemed to require it.

The story of Bartimaeus,
which was feelingly recounted by St. Mark,
tells of a blind beggar of Jericho
who was sadly consigned to the dark,
either by nature or bad luck:
it is not made clear in the scripture
how exactly he came to endure
the rather limiting strictures
of sightlessness. We are told only
that he was disruptive, a bother.
When he heard the man who taught us
when we pray to say, "Our Father"
was in the neighbourhood,
Blind Bartimaeus began to whine and plead.
Jesus, fed up with his complaining, said
"Enough!" he said, "tell me what you need!"
"My sight!" said the beggar,
whom the doctors described as a hopeless case.
"Then it's yours," said the rabbi,
"I give you wholeness because you have faith."

61

This is what the Gospels say.
And that was the story that came to mind
when they realized their goat —
a newborn male — was, in fact, blind.
Now, most male goats aren't allowed to linger:
that's the awful truth of it.
They're usually destined for
an early rendezvous with the spit,
and a slow carousel spin above
a bed of glowing coals.
They're just not good for much. And if they're blind?
Well — the writing's on the wall.
His span on earth was sure to be short:
still, he would require a name.
So they called him Bartimaeus,
like the beggar of Biblical fame:
Timmy for short, as it was
a cumbersome handle for a kid to bear.
Then they set him loose with the other goats,
To forge some kind of career.

To everyone's surprise, but his own,
he acquitted himself rather well.
No one, not knowing his situation,
would be able to tell
That he was in any way different from
his cloven-footed peers.
He frolicked, he gamboled,
And his disposition was such that he endeared
himself to everyone who met him
with his intelligence, his charm.
His keepers, who after all knew goats from goats,
were thoroughly disarmed.
They admired his keenness, his enthusiasm,
admired his confident stance,
admired his guile when he made his escapes,
and his overall insouciance.
They forgot he couldn't see the world —
not even through a darkening glass;
and when slaughter season came,
his brothers went. But Timmy? The angel passed.

We know, of course, about scapegoats:
how an animal was sacrificed
to wash away the sins that somehow accrue
over the course of a life.
Poor goats, is what I say:
held aloft before the crowd, their opened veins
spilling cleansing blood so we could go
and sin the same sins yet again.
I rather like to think their souls,
sundered from wasted flesh, survived;
and that, watchful, they contrived
to keep Bartimaeus the goat alive:
a cosmic conspiracy,
and also, sort of a lesson
regarding the folly of passing harsh judgement
based on initial impressions.
Sad ghosts of goats, we charge you to hover
Above him, beside him, around:
Straighten the path that Bartimaeus walks,
Glad, blind goat, and God's sweetest clown.

HESTER AND THE WHALE

This is an example of Mr. Richardson's juvenilia, included primarily for the benefit of those scholars who see The Bard as dissertation material. This is, in fact, his very first Cautionary Tale. It has raised the ire of environmental activists, who must also rage whenever they read Jonah or Pinocchio.

Hester was a tranquil child,
Sweet, soft-spoken, meek and mild,
Seldom seen and never heard:
She rarely dared to speak a word
For fear it might lodge in the craw
Of her Papa and her Maman.
She listened to each thing they said
And gladly did as she was bade.
Rebellion never crossed her mind —
It could be messy and unkind,
And Hester would at any price
Endeavour to be neat and nice.
One day, Maman and Hester listened
To the fishing expedition
Plans that Papa'd gone and made.
He'd booked the tickets and had paid
A large sum for their deep-sea spree
To an exclusive agency.

"They promise it will be a lark!
We shall see dolphins, squid and sharks.
And though these trappings cost me dear —
The flippers, snorkels and the spears —
Let's think about our fish-filled freezer!"
Maman smiled. The prospect pleased her.
Hester frankly didn't think
Three weeks upon the briny drink
Would be a jolly holiday.
She couldn't bring herself to say
That she was troubled by the thought
Of how the threesome might be caught
Quite unprepared in parts remote
By mighty whales in their small boat.
But caution would just spoil the fun,
She kept the peace and held her tongue.

Thus Hester found herself at sea
With her Maman and Papa. She
Tried by day to smile and beam,
By night tried to ignore her dreams:
Dreams in which she'd thrash and flail,
Dreams of Christmases in whales.
Maman and Papa one day donned
Masks and flippers, then were gone,
Ignorant of Hester's grief,
To photograph a coral reef.
Hester watched them swim to port,
Saw them gambol, saw them sport,
Then leaning o'er the starboard rail
She saw — oh! Was it? — Yes! A whale!

ester was a tranquil child...

Where could she run? Where could she flee?
It saw her simultaneously,
And knew that with but little tussle
It could procure a tasty morsel.
Back to port sweet Hester scurried,
Brow now etched with lines of worry.
Should she summon to her aid
Her parents dear? Papa had paid
The agency a fearsome sum:
She could not, would not ruin their fun —
So cautious Hester rested mum.

Within the hour her folks returned,
Content, if oh so slightly burned.
The sun was hot. They smiled and yawned.
They did not notice she was gone
Till three weeks later back on shore.
Maman wept. Her heart was sore.
Papa consoled and reassured:
"There, there dear. She *was* insured."
This story has a moral, of course.
You'll suffer Hester's fate or worse:
If you neglect to speak your mind —
You'll be the lunch some whale finds.

urtis headed home from school and
dawdled on his way…

Soothing The Savage Beast

Mr. Richardson was asked to write a child-accessible poem in order to encourage a young man named Curtis in his piano practice. The petitioner was Curtis's granny, and The Poet was glad to oblige. He himself has inscribed "abandoning the piano" at the tippy-top of his very considerable list of regrets.

Curtis headed home from school and dawdled on his way,
His face was frozen in a kind of glower.
When all his friends were finally freed to run and shout and play,
He wrestled the piano for an hour.

Each day he had to sit astride the hard revolving stool,
Each day he had to practice without fail.
Each day it was the same routine when he came in from school:
First the major, then the minor scales.

Each day he had to memorize a little piece by Bach,
Or Mozart, or another of that crowd.
His grandma watched his progress with the keenness of a hawk;
She told him that one day he'd make her proud.

"When you grow up, you'll thank me," she would tell him when he whined,
"To have a skill you ought not be without!
Music is the food of love, and love can be sublime!"
"I think love sucks!" said Curtis, with a pout.

Now on the day of which I speak, as Curtis scuffed along —
Not eager in the slightest to begin —
He paused beside a manhole and, as he was feeling strong,
He pried the cover off and bellowed in:

"Is anybody home?" he called. His question echoed deep.
"Is anybody home?" came back again.
He bellowed in the sewer, "Go and take a flying leap!"
A hand reached up and pulled him down the drain.

He had no time to call for help or raise a loud alarm,
He passed from light to darkness in a trice.
He found himself encircled by a slimy, scaly arm:
Strong as a gorilla, cold as ice.

All was gloom and smelliness. They made a fast descent,
The atmosphere was dangerous and rank.
They veered along canals that seemed, no matter where they went,
Cold and clammy, dismal, dark, and dank.

Now, you might well suspect that Curtis felt a tad distressed,
He didn't know by what he'd just been snatched:
He only knew he didn't feel particularly blessed
At having been abducted down the hatch.

What sewer demon held him in this chill and steely grasp?
Was this some evil creature of the night?
When at last they stopped the boy released a startled gasp:
They'd come upon a chamber filled with light.

Chandeliers hung everywhere. A thousand candles burned,
The room they lit had never seen the sun.
It held a lavish table. Curtis very quickly learned
The reason it was only set for one.

"Of course, you'll stay for dinner," were the words his captor said,
And all about the room that sentence rang.
Curtis turned and took him in. His eyes were brilliant red:
Red as well, the stains upon his fangs.

Eyes and fangs and scales and tail and breath to make you swoon,
And hair that hung about in twisted coils:
The creature said, "Sit down. Relax. I'm having dinner soon.
You're small and shouldn't take too long to boil.

"My microwave is broken, but the kettle's working well.
There'll only be the shortest of delays.
In the meantime, have a seat and visit for a spell —
Unless, of course, you think you'd like to play?"

He gestured to the corner where a grand piano stood.
Curtis felt a sudden sense of calm.
He said, "Why, yes, I'll play a while. My granny says I'm good.
Perhaps you'd like to hear a bit of Brahms?"

The demon clapped his filthy paws, with loud delight he trilled,
"Brahms! My favourite! What a clever guy!"
Curtis sat and summoned up his every ounce of will:
He played the very famous lullaby.

"Charming!" said the demon. Curtis played it one time through,
He played it twice, then version three and four:
He played it several dozen times, for in his heart he knew
Eventually he'd hear the demon snore.

"How lovely!" said his captor, as his lids began to sag.
"Divine!" he said while covering a yawn.
"Oh dear," he said, "I must confess, I feel a trifle bagged!
"I'll rest my eyes..." In seconds, he was gone.

Enterprising Curtis rose, then quickly as he dared
He fled the room and plunged into the black,
He only thought to gain sufficient distance from the lair:
He never once considered looking back.

He followed awful corridors, he twisted left and right,
He prayed a prayer and never words were truer,
Asking for deliverance from the creature of the night,
Rescue from the Phantom of the Sewer.

To make a long, long story short — he found that selfsame hole.
He scuttled up, and hurried down the street.
Squinting in the sunlight like a subterranean mole,
And smelling far from what you might call sweet.

And from that day to this one he has practiced without fail.
When next he meets a beast whose feet are cloven,
He'll know a dozen lullabies to charm him and regale:
Schumann, Schubert, Mozart and Beethoven.

Oh what can be more glorious than belting out a song?

Joyful Noises

The Bard is possessed of a truly glorious singing voice. Alas, he is surrounded by Philistines who fail to recognize his world class instrument for what it is, and are forever telling him to shush. Herein lies the inspiration for this poem, which he dedicates to every other Orpheus who has been silenced by the rabble.

Oh what can be more glorious than belting out a song?
To hear a well-loved chorus and to start to sing along?
When voices make the welkin ring all's right and nothing's wrong,
We're happy: every woman, child and man!
But anyone who's spent a week or maybe two at school
Will know that here and there you find exceptions to the rule,
And surely as the eight-ball is the centrepiece of pool,
I cite you Etta May and Flora Ann.

Etta May adored to sing. She loved to lift her voice,
And tune her high soprano, trilling Handel's glad "Rejoice!"
But Flora Ann, her sister, always bellowed "Cut the noise!
You're sounding like the neighbour's cat in heat!
Who told you you knew how to sing? That horrid little squawk
Sounds nothing like a nightingale and mighty like a hawk."
Thus would nasty Flora Ann revile, defile and mock
Both rude and crude and wholly indiscreet.

The truth is she was jealous. Etta's light and lyric lilt,
If given half a chance could make an opera lover wilt,
Or stir the bonny billows of a Scotsman's tartan kilt:
She had a treasure buried in her throat.
But Flora could not bear to see her gifted sibling shine
When Etta pitched her pipes the bitter Flora would opine
That music this was not, but just a reedy little whine:
She'd make her sister mute, and then she'd gloat.

But then one day it happened, as in old medieval days,
A dragon came to town: the kind that knights in armour slay,
But knights were rather scarce, and so the dragon simply stayed
To wreak a path of havoc wide and deep;
He seemed possessed of every vile reptilian psychosis,
His fiery breath was worse than Uncle Barney's halitosis,
And all the nervous damsels felt the dawning of neurosis,
And by and large were troubled in their sleep.

Now Flora, who was nasty, went with Etta, who was good,
To gather nuts and berries in the very scary woods.
They didn't really want to go, they didn't think they should,
But woe is me! The cupboard shelves were bare.
They filled their wicker basket to the brim with nature's gifts
And Etta, in the moment, felt her flagging spirits lift.
She raised her pretty voice in song: the consequence was swift,
They felt the dragon's breath and saw his stare.

"Yikes!" said frightened Flora when she saw the looming thing,
"Oy!" exclaimed her sister at the scales and nails and wings,
The dragon, inarticulate, reared up and roared, "Who sing?"
He hovered on the cusp of being peeved.
Or so it seemed to Flora, who herself was feeling riled,
She pointed to her sister, little Etta, meek and mild,
"She did! She's the culprit! She's a vicious, spiteful child!"
Her breathing came in spurts, her bosom heaved.

Evil-minded Flora tossed her long and curly mane.
"Eat her up," she blustered, "so that none of us again
Have to hear her singing! Do it! Spare us future pain!
Toast her and I swear I'll never tell!"
Then the fearsome dragon opened up his gaping maw,
Roared his fearsome roar and showed his long and fearsome claws,
Spouted molten spittle from his hinged and awful jaws —
The scene approximated deepest Hell.

Flora, when the smoke had cleared, was nowhere to be found,
Unless of course you count the heap of ash upon the ground.
Etta and the dragon sang a happy little round,
"Frère Jacques" perhaps, or "Row, row, row."
The dragon, it transpired, was a fan of vocal art —
He loved to sing the harmonies, the bass or tenor part,
And Etta's tuneful crooning touched his overheated heart,
And now the two have got a traveling show.

The fans and critics love them, which is easy to explain:
Given Flora's fate, who'd have the moxy to complain?
Brimstone waits for those who dare to rub against the grain,
Who would care to take the team to task?
So, let this be a warning then, to all who grouse and cringe:
When someone starts to sing, recall how close sing is to singe;
Receive their songs with joy and don't belittle, gripe or winge!
The dragon waits for whom? You needn't ask.

From time to time one meets a soul
who pays but little heed…

Haggis Wrestling

Man against beast! Ever since Beowulf, this has been a popular theme for epic poems. This is a contemporary epic, suitable for public reading around Robbie Burns day.

From time to time one meets a soul who pays but little heed
To trite conventionality, who spits on caution's creed.
I don't mean folks like you and me who never fail to floss,
And never think of saying things like "Shove it" to the boss.
Our way of sweeping up the days induces gaping yawns
In those the gods of derring-do have blessed and smiled upon:
The rogues who ride their motorbikes on seldom-traveled paths,
And care not if they close the door when lounging in the bath.

They like to put on parachutes and chuck themselves from planes:
Comport themselves as if they're certifiably insane.
Of all the great daredevils though, there's none that can compare
With those of whom I mean to sing, the rarest of the rare.
If they were all assembled, they'd not constitute a throng:
You may well not have heard of them in ballad or in song.
Oh who? Oh who? I hear you cry, Oh who? Oh who? Oh who?
Oh tell us, tell us, tell us now, oh tell us, tell us do!

Then since you beg, I'll condescend to say that I allude
To those whose avocation strikes the faint of heart as crude.
So know that I refer to those whose unrepentant bag is
Leaping in a wrestling ring to there assail a haggis.
Yes! Haggis wrestlers are the subject of this fervent hymn:
These brawny nutters regularly risk both life and limb
To entertain their fans and extricate them from life's rut
By going to the limit with a mass of trussed, stuffed gut.

It goes like this: MacTavish slips between the square rings ropes,
Acknowledges the plaudits: he is full of vim and hope.
Some sweet-faced granny cups her hands to lips and then she cries:
"Kill the slimy bastard, Mac! But first gouge out his eyes!"
MacTavish raises up his hands, and shakes them o'er his head,
Betraying not the slightest trace of terror, fear or dread.
But then a hush falls on the room. The crowd exhales an "OOOH!"
At witnessing the entrance of coagulated goo —

An oozing, pocked excrescence, sausage round, intestine grey:
You'd have to be a fool to bet this slime could win the day.
MacTavish seems bemused to see his foul opponent sag.
He laughs the laugh of one who thinks he has it in the bag.
The crowd is calling out for blood. MacTavish paws and snorts,
"Och aye" he sighs, and slaps his thighs. "It won't be real sport."
He lunges for the haggis! Everybody stands and roars!
The two opponents start to roll about the canvas floor.

"You nasty bit of work," he snarls, "I'll shortly hear you beg!"
He tries his trusty leg hold, but he cannot find a leg.
He finds as well his armlock and his toe hold both are useless;
His never-fail half-Nelson and his head clamp both prove toothless.
His hands are thick with goop. He finds he cannot keep a grip.
He's fit and strong and eager, but his best manoeuvres slip.
The audience has sensed a change. They swill their tepid beer:
Each time the haggis slides away, they raise a louder cheer.

"Let him have it, Haggy!" cries the granny, fit to bust.
Everyone is sharing of her dark, primeval lust:
Lust for blood and lust for bone, they beg the pulsing mass
To end it all by dealing out a killing *coup de grâce*.
MacTavish is exhausted now. He's prostrate on the mat.
The haggis rears up, stallion-like, to squash the Scotsman flat.
The crowd recoils, they hide their eyes, they hear a crunch and slurp,
And then a heavy slithering, and then a mighty burp.

And when they look again, they see the ring is now devoid
Of any sign of haggis or the Scot that he destroyed.
Where did he go? Where does he live? At what gym does he train?
They ask themselves these questions, but they pose them all in vain.
The haggis has retired for now. He's found a place to nestle.
When Burns Day comes around next year, he'll surface and he'll wrestle.
So be ye warned, dare-mongers, though your boasting may be lavish:
The foe is great. Your date with fate will see you meet MacTavish.

The day does not go by when I'm not given cause to pause...

There's One In Every Eden

This is surely one of The Poet's most celebrated Cautionary Tales. It is based on a true story related to him by Gail Smiley. She and her husband Mike are potters who live in Ontario. Mike has an aversion to serpents and their kin, Gail has a keen sense of humour. When a snake somehow slithered into her husband's shorts while they were on a bicycle trip, Gail couldn't wait to share her bemusement with the nation. She forwarded the details to Mr. Richardson who was quick to grasp the Freudian overtones. The Bard says that writing this poem was like following a burning brand to the promised land. Or was that a burning bush? What does it matter? It's a masterpiece!

The day does not go by when I'm not given cause to pause
And wonder how we blunder on, in spite of all our flaws.
We learn to trust our bodies, then discover we're betrayed:
The willing flesh grows poxy and is destined to decay,
And what is more, the spirit, which the sages say is weak,
Often proves the proverb's truth by springing psychic leaks.
Consider, please, the phobia: unreasonable fear.
Some people start to shudder when they know a bat is near,
Some fear mathematics, some fear bees, and some fear heights,
And some can't stand to leave the land to take a cruise or flight.
Some people hate wide spaces, others cannot be confined:
Fear that knows no reason — thus may phobic be defined.

Now, put your feet upon a stool, and take a little break,
And listen to the tale of Mike who can't abide the snake.
He was a true ophidiophobe, for that's the appellation
For one in whom the snake engenders more than consternation.
Poor Mike had no idea how he came to be afflicted:
He only knew his heart would pound, his breathing grow constricted,
His knees would shake, his brow would sweat, his brain and bowels be
    blighted,
The second he suspected that a serpent might be sighted.
Now, one day in September, with his spousal unit, Gail,
Mike propelled his bicycle along a scenic trail.
They passed a lovely garden, and surveyed the sylvan scene,
Surveyed, too, some emporium where one could buy ice cream.

They'd cycled far, the day was hot, and ice cream struck a chord:
They bought themselves a cone apiece and called it their reward.
They sprawled about the garden like a pair of sylphs, or fawns:
Decked out in their shorts they languished on the lavish lawns.
The ice cream was a sensual treat. It set them both to purring,
And Mike detected in his shorts an unaccustomed stirring.
"Here, here, here, what's this?" he asked, now just a tad suspicious,
The cone he ate was good but wasn't potently delicious.
He looked down at his pelvis, and its old familiar charms,
And noted with a measure of distress, indeed, alarm
That something was unsheathed and was revealed in stark protrusion.
Or so he thought initially. Imagine his confusion

At watching as it grew and grew. This brooked no comprehension.
In seconds it surpassed the most conventional dimensions.
Was this some visitation? Such events, Mike knew, were rare,
And this was nothing he had ever mentioned in his prayers.
Mike looked again in wonderment. It did not take him long
To understand that something here was very, very wrong.
His brain fired up its synapses. Fear shook him to the core,
At understanding that, in fact, a snake snuck from his drawers.
Mike leapt up and bellowed out, and danced upon the sod:
"A snake, a snake, a snake!" he cried. "My God, my God, my God!"
I know that there are questions here that beg investigation,
That all your curiosities cry out for satiation.

You want the why, you want the how. Such queries lead to quibbling.
Let's just suppose the snake sought out a small and long-lost sibling,
And as the thing was cunning, wily, slippery, and determined
It found a way. It could not know Mike looked on snakes as vermin.
It could not in its reptile brain have harboured the perception
That it would find not refuge, but a hostile, riled reception.
It felt, as it slip-slithered off, a little like a martyr:
A garter snake denied the chance to function as a garter.
Poor Mike! His day was drained of any chance for further fun,
He danced the tarantella of his trauma in the sun.
And thus concludes the tragic tale, told out in manner strophic:
A cautionary verse for all devout ophidiophobics.

There is ample evidence, no matter where one turns...

When Biorhythms Call, Answer

The observant reader will have noticed that we are now into a run of poems concerning men. Mr. Richardson, being a man, feels a deep sense of connection with these works. Here he tackles the thorny and sensitive issue of the male menopause. The Bard knows whereof he speaks, as he has been hosting such a condition since he was fourteen.

There is ample evidence, no matter where one turns,
That rhythm, first and foremost, is the shaper of our days.
Nature is a metronome, as every schoolchild learns:
The sun and moon are regimental with their beams and rays,
Planets whirl like clockwork through the stars, ranged rank on rank,
And every day the tides deposit treasures on the shore,
And then sneak back again, like thieves, to rob those selfsame banks.
Everything has rhythm. Who could ask for something more?

Within each body's kingdom too, are tidal tugs and shifts:
There's menses, peristalsis, and the whole circadian band
That bangs its drums and tambourines as through our days we drift —
The thudding heart's the governor who oversees the land.
As we enter middle age, these corporal rhythms change.
Woman's life by swinging mood and torrid flash is marred.
Man, as well, it's plain to see, begins to act deranged,
Running off with mistresses, and buying stupid cars.

What exactly happens is both subtle and profound;
There's something deep inside that snaps, and takes a dreadful toll.
Rudderless, we founder and proceed to run aground.
Gregory, of whom I sing, swore he'd retain control.
Gregory was cognizant of Nature's heinous plan,
So Gregory, at thirty-five, grew vigilant and shrewd,
Vowing up and down that he'd not be the kind of man
Who'd buy a red Miata, or engage in conduct lewd.

Gregory vowed up and down to steer a steady course,
And never let his biorythmic urges run amuck.
All his friends and colleagues fell to chaos and divorce:
He watched them purchase motorbikes and fuchsia pick-up trucks,
Watched them hire clinicians who can graft hair back on scalps,
And watched while plastic surgeons lyposucked their gross excess,
Saw them drain their savings and go skiing in the Alps,
And saw their many girlfriends in a state of semi-dress.

All his stiff-necked rectitude would put to shame the Pope.
Though rebel stirrings troubled him, he never let them flower.
Rather, he would nip them in the bud, and he could cope
With black and heated lustiness by taking frigid showers.
Every time he felt an urge or longing untoward,
Gregory would doff his duds and brave the icy spray.
Outside, in the wicked world, his friends caroused and whored,
But Gregory, for all intents and purposes, was spayed.

Gregory was neutered by this self-inflicted chill,
And though his mid-life longings grew increasingly intense,
He would not give in to them. He fortified his will
With hours and hours of showers as his principal defence.
Eventually, it did him in. His terrible regime
Of chill self-deprivation brought about his sad demise.
They found him wet and frowning. At his funeral, it seems,
The mourners, by and large, were smiling forty-something guys.

Dear ones, take this tale to heart, and heed life's rhythms well:
They cannot be anaesthetized, and will not be assuaged.
Greet the scheduled crazies with a friendly "What the hell!"
And sow your wild oats happily throughout your middle age.
Sow your wild oats happily, cull rosebuds while you can!
Oh, think of oats and rosebuds now, for you can surely bet
When your middle years are done, if you employ this plan
You'll giggle through your golden years with nothing to regret.

The story I'll tell you is all about Al...

Nothing Like A Dame

All right, men! Hands up! How many of you have tried on a frock when no one was looking? Oh, don't fret. It was just a phase. Here is a little verse about a man called Al who went a bit over the top. Mr. Richardson is acquainted with a number of night clubs where Al might find lasting happiness.

The story I'll tell you is all about Al,
A mountainous man who had mountainous pals,
With gym-sculpted bodies unsullied by toxins:
Their calves hard as granite and necks thick as oxen,
With hillocks for chests and with statuesque shoulders
And biceps the size of conventional boulders,
With tummies that rippled and thighs made of thunder,
And as for the rest — well, I'll leave you to wonder.

They all had Camaros emblazoned with dragons,
And brows anthropologists might call Cro-Magnon.
In every way masculine in their deportment:
Oh, never was seen such a macho assortment.
Hallowe'en night was again on the verge
And Al and his pals had the fun-loving urge
To deck themselves out and do something inane.
"I got it," Al ventured. "Let's go out as dames!"

"Yeah! Dames!" said his buddies. "Va va va va voom!"
One snickered, "Hooters!" One chuckled, "Bazooms!"
They drove to the thrift store and swiftly took stock,
They bought hideous wigs and rebarbative frocks,
They tried on the shoes and like madmen careened
From pillar to post in their pumps, size 16.
They dashed to the cash and unloaded their carts,
Then went home to practice the womanly arts.

Big Al, on arrival, made haste to put on
His black *crêpe de Chine* and his hot pink chiffon.
He looked in the mirror and liked what he saw:
His nice way with scarves, his complexion *sans* flaw.
He was big, he was butch, and devotedly hetero...
But still he was thrilled to be sporting stilettoes.
He felt like a diva: Tebaldi or Callas.
Thus Al was transformed, and before him stood Alice.

He stood breathing heavily, misting the mirror,
He lurched back a step, teetered nearer and nearer,
And then just as surely as push leads to shove
Allan and Alice fell deeply in love.
Yes, surely as borrowers look for a lender
Al was enmeshed in confusion of gender,
And surely as knickknacks belitter a shelf
Big Al, at a glance, fell in love with himself.

Hallowe'en came, they all had a great time,
And when it was over his buddies consigned
Their dresses and girdles, their borroweds and blues
To attics and basements and Sally Anns, too.
Al though, was different. His buddies were stumped
To see him keep purchasing boas and pumps.
His father was puzzled, his mother depressed,
But Al wanted Alice dependably dressed.

Psychologists doubtless could try to explain,
And give Al's condition a clinical name,
Reveal how his fondness for ladies' emporia
Signals some kind of a gender dysphoria,
Call him regressive, or else narcissistic.
Labels, however, are simply simplistic.
Al thinks his life has been latterly great.
He never again needs to look for a date.

A touch of mascara, a girdle and bra,
A dress, matching pumps with a clutch and *voila!*
In just half an hour he's changed and he's ready.
Alice and Al, quite content going steady.
Perhaps you will think this is simply absurd,
Dismiss as apocryphal what you have heard.
All fellows, at some point, on some Hallowe'en
Will smear up their faces with mom's Maybelline,

Will put on her shoes, even colour their hair
And next day are nothing the worse for the wear.
So why then should Al, quintessentially normal,
Now go out to restaurants bedecked in a formal?
He just knows for certain that self-dating's fun,
He's Al and he's Alice: a couple in one.
The moral is simple. I close with this lone word.
Dateless this weekend? Then angel, look homeward.

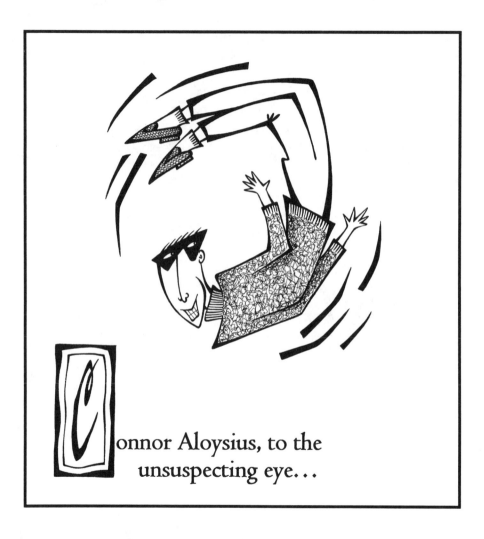

onnor Aloysius, to the
unsuspecting eye...

Given Up For Lint

How lamentable that the geniuses from whose creative minds sprang full-formed such useful collecting devices as the Toaster Crumb Tray and, especially, the Dryer Lint Trap, have gone unheralded. The Poet, who can be seen in some of the toniest laundromats of downtown Vancouver, particularly regrets that so few of his countrymen and women see fit to honour the Dryer Lint Trap by according it the courtesy of emptying it. This poem is aimed directly at these laggards. Duck!

Connor Aloysius, to the unsuspecting eye,
Was the very picture of an average kind of guy.
There was nothing untoward about his dress or mien:
Neat in every habit and conventionally lean,
Not in any way encumbered with alarming quirks,
Always paid his tax on time, and never late for work,
Opened doors for seniors, always watched his Ps and Qs.
Need a word to sum him up? It's "normalcy" you'd choose.
There was nothing like a sign, no outward clue or hint
To indicate his lusty love for handling dryer lint.

Who's to say just how this strange pathology began?
It lived within his psyche long before he was a man.
Perhaps when Connor Aloysius languished in the womb
Mama's innards rumbled like a happy laundry room,
Engendering within her son, curled up in foetal lair,
Associations that persisted after sucking air:

Comfort and security, a blissful sense of peace,
Reinforced in adulthood by handling bits of fleece.
Speculations such as this are wholly academic:
Somehow, love of lint in Aloysius was endemic.

Love of lint was in him. That is all we need to know.
Love of lint took over as the boy began to grow.
Innocent enough at first, he'd watch the dryer spin.
When the cycle finished he would gleefully reach in,
Grab the brimming lint trap, sing a glad and praiseful psalm,
Rubbing toasty clothing dross in finger and palm:
"I shall lift mine eyes," he'd sing, "to lint, joy's total sum!"
"My, how strange," his ma would say. But there was worse to come.
Soon her dryer's output couldn't satisfy his needs.
Lint! He needed lint, like junkies hunger after speed.

Connor Aloysius started going door to door
Asking of the neighbours favours never asked before.
"Clean your lint trap, lady?" he'd beseech each startled *frau*.
Bringing lines of puzzlement to every worried brow.
This request seemed so bizarre that most of them declined.
Therefore Connor Aloysius turned his hand to crime.
Late at night, when all was still, he'd go out on a spree,
Connor Aloysius grew adept at B & E's:
Dressed in black, his face obscured by mask and jaunty cap,
He would risk arrest to scoop the lint from out the trap.

Lint and lint and lint again! His longing ruined his life.
How could he sustain a friendship, hope to keep a wife?
Finally his lusting drove him clear around the bend,
Brought him to a sad and sorry sordid kind of end.
Oh, he should have seen the light! He should have sworn the pledge!
One day in the laundromat, he stepped right off the edge.
He opened up a dryer, and he stuffed himself inside,
Fed it quarters, slammed the door, and tumbled till he fried.
What a messy outcome to his strange, untrammelled lust!
Lint to lint is not as nice, alas, as dust to dust.

Where is Aloysius now? I fear he's with us yet.
As a ghost he longs for lint, as much as he can get.
Haunting every laundry room where lazy washday saps
Finish with the dryers, then neglect to clean the traps.
Therefore, I suggest unless you want to host a ghost,
When your laundry's freshly dried and still as warm as toast,
Clean the bloody lint trap out! Leave not to linger there
Remnants of your laundry — bits of fluff and curly hair.
Clean the bloody lint trap out! Thus ends my warning verse.
Connor Aloysius died, and your fate could be worse.

Often have I heard it said, by wisdom-sated sages...

Hedging Her Bets

Some human impulses, such as the writing of Poetry, or the illustrating of Poetry, are laudable. Others, such as the urge to make a shrub resemble something it is not, are incomprehensible. Topiary has always befuddled The Poet, and here he vents his befuddlement.

Often have I heard it said, by wisdom-sated sages,
That angels are our guardians as through our days we drift.
Likewise have I read forgotten lore on tattered pages,
Attributing to angels the disbursement of our gifts.
We are simply banks, you see, the angels count upon
For saving gifts eternal that will one day be passed on.

In banks of blood and flesh and bone they make their safe deposits,
Squirreling gifts away until our time on earth is done.
Some folks let their talents hang and moulder in the closet,
Others wave them proudly, just like banners in the sun.
Some folks wave them proudly, others lock them in a tower.
Angels give us gifts: the choice to use them, though, is ours.

Every gift we're given ought to properly be coddled:
That's a glowing tenet that we ought to take to heart.
But this trusty maxim was — I feel quite certain — modeled,
With in mind a talent, say, for music or for art.
Music, art and science all are pleasing to behold;
Other gifts, alas, can cast their owners in the cold.

Cynthia, for instance, had an angel who was addled,
Somewhat short on taste, who inexplicably was pleased
When he handed talents out to see his client saddled
With a burning lust for sculpting shrubbery and trees.
Woe betide the angel then who found it in his heart
To lay upon poor Cynthia the topiarist's art!

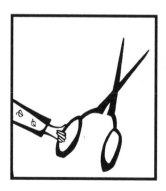

Topiary was her gift. While still bedecked in pampers
Cynthia took shears in hand and laid into the shrubs,
Eager to effect their transformation, off she scampered!
Well before the child was weaned and eating solid grub,
Cynthia turned bush to squirrel: the evil seeds were sown.
"When," bemoaned her folks, "can we, in decency, disown?"

Prodigy and prodigal, and terrorizing tyrant,
Anything with leaf and branch would prompt the child to snip.
Grandma's rhododendron was transmogrified to hydrant,
Then her favourite rosebush was denuded of its hips.
Cynthia removed the hips, and branch or two and lo!
Where the rose had been she left a fragrant bear to grow.

Her parents were disturbed at this, and sought expensive guidance:
Eighty bucks an hour they paid a psychiatric corps,
Just to hear them mutter words like "trauma" and "avoidance."
When at last the puzzled shrink would show them to the door,
Outside in the waiting room was Cynthia, enthralled,
Trimming deifenbachias in answer to her call.

Just like little Washington, she would not stoop to lying:
"It was I!" she'd crow when they'd confront her with her crimes:
Life with little Cynthia grew every day more trying.
Finally her parents knew they'd run clean out of time.
Unable to restrain their child, or train her to be good,
They made her wear a blindfold and they left her in the woods.

Just like Gretel's parents they assumed that she was done for,
Thought she'd be devoured by a loathsome, hungry beast.
Cynthia, however, looked around and soon found comfort.
She was quite alone, but wasn't worried in the least.
Au contraire, she found a stand of trees to call a hedge,
And Cynthia pushed topiary to the cutting edge.

Cynthia, mad Cynthia, alone and unobstructed,
Snipped from trees a castle with a throne room and a moat.
In the moat swam hungry sharks, of juniper constructed,
Sharks with thorny teeth to slice an unsuspecting throat.
For a solid week she toiled and laboured in her wood.
Finally she looked around and saw that it was good.

Horses made of leaf and branch are tethered in her stable,
Courtiers carved from holly fill her ivy-covered halls.
So we reach the moral of this topiary fable:
Solitary Cynthia is happy, overall.
Make your gift your castle, friend, and if the mob recoils,
Lift the drawbridge, flash a finger, boil a pot of oil.

nce, not very long ago, a man
whom we'll call Ted…

Read or Digest

During his teenage years, The Bard spent hours and hours locked in the bathroom. When asked what he was doing therein, he replied, "Reading." Now, he feels that he can confess that he was, in fact, reading. This caused considerable inconvenience, and even discomfort, to others in his family. Mr. Richardson sends this Cautionary Tale out to them, with his apologies.

Once, not very long ago, a man whom we'll call Ted
Fell in love with Brenda and in time's due course, they wed.
They had a tiny, perfect house upon a quiet street,
Where every hedge was nicely trimmed and every lawn was neat,
Where nothing broke the quiet but the sprinkler's genial hiss.
Ted's and Brenda's lives, in short, were deeply steeped in bliss.

Deeply steeped in sweetest bliss were Ted's and Brenda's lives:
Their soufflés never withered and their every houseplant thrived,
They paid off all their credit cards and bills when they came due:
Oh! But they were happy in their Eden made for two!
But surely as the Volvo is the favoured car of Sweden,
Look around and you will find a serpent in each Eden.

Serpents are ingredients in Eden's old prescription.
Ted and Brenda's serpent was a cherished gift subscription.
Readers' Digest reached them on a steady, monthly basis.
Throughout the land that chronicle's accorded honoured places:
By sofa or by bedside, if we mention merely two.
Ted and Brenda's *Readers' Digest* languished in the loo.

In the loo their monthly *Digest* waited to be read,
Enlivening the private times of Brenda and of Ted.
Never, while they dealt with their respective constitutions
Would they ever suffer from ennui in mid-ablution.
"How to Save Your Marriage" or "The Pancreas of Joe":
Every page contained some snippet everyone should know.

On each page a snippet on eradicating stains,
Reports on analgesics for the management of pain,
Tales of true adventure, reminiscences of war,
Countless feeble jokes they'd heard a thousand times before.
Glory! What a treasure trove! Beloved of the throng!
Month grew into month, and bathroom sessions grew prolonged.

Hubby was the first to rise, while Brenda rested prone.
Ted would use the bathroom first, and perch upon the throne.
Once ensconced he pulled a volume from the looming pile:
"Life's Like That" would always make him chuckle, make him smile.
Ted would sit there reading for a half an hour or more,
By which time his loving spouse was pounding on the door.

Ted who'd yet to shower, and who hadn't brushed or flossed,
Had to rise so Brenda could recuperate time lost.
She would, in her turn, sit down upon the seat he'd warmed,
Pick a *Digest* up and read the history of corn,
Or possibly a tragic tale, a flood, a missing child.
Meanwhile, Ted was at the door, and sounding pretty riled.

"We'll both be late for work!" She would precipitously rise,
Having learned another way to trim and slim her thighs,
And then there came a flurry as they finished their toilettes:
Flailing razors, hurried showers, mumblings of regret.
And since they'd just one bathroom, every morning there arose
Congestion 'round the toothpaste and the treading on of toes.

This went on and on and on. Each new day made it worse:
Their bathroom time grew longer, their discussions grew more terse,
Their playful, carefree banter had a vitriolic edge:
Their love of *Readers' Digest* had become a sharpened wedge.
Brenda read an article called "Why Your Mate's A Jerk."
Ted left open, by the toilet, "Can Your Marriage Work?"

Tension is like floorwax: when you heap it, layer on layer,
It leads to nasty build-ups, and to slippery places where
Unwary souls might tumble, and be injured by the fall:
Which brings us back to Eden, where we started after all.
Ted and Brenda's Paradise was ruptured on the day
Ted, while reading in the john, decided he would stay.

Who's to say just why he cracked and boarded up the door?
Brenda hammered feelingly, as she had done before.
Ted refused to answer her. She pleaded and she whined.
Through the barricaded door he muttered, "Mine! All mine!"
This was just too much to bear. His sad, beleaguered wife,
Called the local firemen to bring the jaws of life.

Ted was dragged away and labelled "psychically corrupted."
Brenda hardly misses him. She reads uninterrupted.
All ye bathroom readers then should from this tale deduce
Excessiveness in this regard can knock a few screws loose.
But if you must confine yourself therein to read at least,
Make it *Readers' Digest* friends. Don't make it *War and Peace*.

In old Elizabethan times,
a clergyman...

Mater = Martyr

Even in these post-feminist times, otherwise intelligent women of a certain age allow themselves to be made into doormats in the service of their families. As a Slave of the Muse, The Poet understands this impulse only too well. Here, he cautions against giving into it — at least, for any reason less vaunted than the service of Art.

In old Elizabethan times, a clergyman — John Foxe —
Wrote of those whose principles could not be sold or bartered,
And who, for standing firm were burned, interned, or clapped in stocks:
His tome is known as *Foxe's Book of Martyrs.*

A modern martyrologist, if one should come along,
Would be enraged to find our age is largely unencumbered
With similarly stalwart souls, whom Foxe saw in their throngs:
Long gone the days of martyrs without number.

But, here and there you find them yet: for instance, Mary Lou.
This poor sad thing of whom I sing, though yet among the living,
Is camped upon the sod that's trod by just the blessed few:
Her tale is broached as we approach Thanksgiving.

Sweet Mary Lou is sixty-nine. Her children number four,
Each made haste to procreate as soon as they were married.
On Sundays and on festive days they thunder through her door:
The pattern, long established, never varies.

Her offspring and her in-laws and their sundry squalling spawn
Thunder to the dining room and range around her table,
And eat the meal that Mary Lou's been whipping up since dawn,
Then bolt like horses from a burning stable.

They do not pause to lend a hand, to gather up the plates:
To clear away the clutter or repair the kiddies' damage,
From time to time, they think to say, "Thanks mama, that was great,
We'll drop around the next time that we're famished."

Her husband, as they flee the house, lies down to take a nap.
Mary Lou ploughs on and never wonders why she chooses
Exactly why — excuse my French — to tolerate this crap:
She's once more in the lurch while hubby snoozes.

But Mary Lou's a martyr, and a martyr it is plain,
Is virtually impervious to anything like reason:
They thrive, like sadomasochists, on cruel abuse and pain,
Regardless of the day or month or season.

Sunday is Thanksgiving. She's been shopping for a week,
On the day, arrive what may, she'll stuff and truss the fowl,
Bake the pies, and squash and yams, and trim and scrub the leeks,
And in the bathroom hang fresh-laundered towels.

The locust will descend, like one of Jeremiah's plagues —
Though when the turkey comes they're more like ravenous piranha —
Intent on stripping all the meat from every wing and leg,
Like lions on the African savanna.

Rip and tear and salivate and belch and chew and rend,
Thump and bang and bark and crash and tatter, fray and clatter,
Gripe and fight the livelong night and bicker without end,
Leave a mess, get up, get dressed, and scatter.

Mary Lou, long suffering, who shops and cooks and carves,
Mary Lou, the martyr, thin as any wraith or fish bone,
She who feeds the multitude but lets herself be starved,
Hangs to dry another gristly wishbone.

Let us wish for Mary Lou that she might see the light,
Turn her back on arid land and choose to graze in clover.
Let us wish that on some near and future Sunday night,
Mary Lou will tell the jerks it's over.

Let us wish that when they raise a loud collective whine,
Mary Lou will stand her ground and make this declaration:
"Stick it where the morning sun is disinclined to shine."
Similarly, all across the nation,

May every martyred mother let her flesh no more be flayed,
May her halo tarnish, may she swear no more to buff it,
Let us wish that when the hordes descend she'll simply say:
"Darlings — here's the turkey. Go and stuff it."

ow pleased I was to bid adieu once
more to Christmas time…

A No Hobby Lobby

The Poet here cries out against all those who feel it is their mission in life to organize his recreational time by presenting him with craft projects in which he has no interest. Stop it, please.

How pleased I was to bid adieu once more to Christmas time,
To see the browning evergreen to crackling flames consigned.
The holly decks the closet where I keep my wrecked umbrellas,
The season left us full of fowl, and free of salmonella.

And all the guests have come and gone, the thank-you notes are written.
I've said, "You really shouldn't have! I'm pleased, I'm chuffed, I'm smitten!"
I've clapped my tiny hands with glee and trilled loud hymns of gratitude,
And treated benefactors to a litany of platitudes.

The truth is that I'd like to know what vile and secret lobby
Tells my friends and family that I'm pining for a hobby.
For every year beneath the tree, as sure as vipers spit,
I'm bound to find some well-intentioned, bloody awful kit.

Just last year I lavished all my smarmy exclamations
On kits for making afghan quilts, and mushroom cultivation.
The quilt is stuck at one inch square, and never shall enfold me,
I tried to grow the mushrooms, but the whole thing went all mouldy.

The clavichord I never built is silent in its box,
The knitting needles never spawned a single pair of socks.
Someone gave me oil paints once. I put them in the cellar
Beside the water colours, and the hook rug kit from Zellers.

I piled them on the jigsaw, underneath the power drill,
Beside the stuff for making wine, plum hootch I'll never swill.
I'd give that wretched cuckoo clock a snowball's chance in hell,
I figure that the candle-making stuff will do as well.

And oh, the paint-by-numbers and the seeds for growing cactus,
And the tinny penny whistle that I'll never ever practice.
It's not that I'm an ingrate, and I'm neither sour nor bitter:
But how can I accommodate the growing heaps of litter?

Have pity on my closets, which on any given day,
Could spill out several hundred tons of twisted macramé,
And likewise might my steamer trunk, on any given week,
Burst its seams and vomit forth an excess of batik.

In another thousand years, or two, or maybe three,
My house will wave a flag of truce to archaeology.
I know some anthropologist will click his heels and cry:
"At last, I've found the site where hobbies crawl away to die!

Oh what an awesome mystery, this enterprising race that
Left behind a broken loom and six half-finished place mats!"
And so, dear friends and relatives, when Christmas comes next year
Don't go out and buy for me a kit for making beer.

If you'd see our bonds endure and prosper, even thrive,
Recollect this mesage when the festive time arrives,
I've only got three interests that require care and feeding:
Get your pencils. Take this down: Smoking. Drinking. Reading.

 like, on Sunday afternoons,
To take the city bus...

The Concert

The Poet is a deeply sensitive man, and his afternoon can be ruined by the slightest infraction of good taste. Here, he rails against those who go to concerts with the express aim of making more noise than the orchestra.

I like, on Sunday afternoons,
To take the city bus,
And hie me to the concert hall,
Abstract me from the fuss
And rush and pell-mell tussle
Of the grim and grimy streets:
Obliterate all ugliness,
Ingest, instead, what's sweet.

I love to hear the orchestra's
Familiar repertoire,
Forget for ninety minutes that
The world's an abattoir,
I like to see the players decked
In tuxes, tails and ties,
And floor-length gowns, discreet and sleek,
So chic! So civilized!

The others in the audience
I know, full well, delight,
To set aside their worries,
Stall the call of gall and spite,
To seek a fragrant Eden
In a land that's ruled by Cain.
But this year there is someone
Who is driving me insane.

Dear lady in the seat next mine,
No doubt you have your charms:
Or so I hope. I often rest
My arm against your arm.
Our separate dermal wrappings brush:
Each concert it's the same.
Skin to skin in dark we sit:
I do not know your name.

Mary, Margaret or Lucille,
Hermione or Claire.
It matters not, nor I to you:
We neither of us care.
Whyever should it matter if
You're Norma, Hilda, Heather?
Or if I'm Tom or Dick or Phil?
We're only brought together

By accident of placement
And, I guess, by common love
Of orchestras and music.
But I swear by Jove above
You're going to drive me bonkers
With the clamour and the din
You seem to feel compelled to make:
Forthwith, a list of sins.

Your handbag is a warehouse
For a plenitude of snacks
Each of which is modest,
Disinclined to shed its wraps.
When finally from the linty depths
Of purse you've pulled and pried
The bonbon that you coveted
You strip its crackly hide.

And when the stubborn cellophane
Has finally been plucked
And wrested from the candy
You are disinclined to suck.
Oh no! You have to chomp this thing!
You've got bionic dentures.
And this is just the outset
Of my sonic misadventures.

I'm sorry you're asthmatic.
You can't help it that you wheeze.
But could you try to moderate
The need to sniff and sneeze?
Resist the urge to let the surge
Of phlegmy, rattling cough
Make the welkin tremble when
The orchestra plays soft.

I think too that you might well find
Your respiratory gloom
Could be alleviated if
You swore off cheap perfume.
And though I cannot claim to be
A medical technician
I'll venture the opinion
That a canny dietitian

Could think of ways to lift you
From your culinary rut,
And thus becalm the rumblings
And the tumblings in your gut.
It's like an Indy racecourse,
And a change in your comestibles
Could surely still the grumbling
In your tract gastrointestinal.

Dear lady in the seat next mine,
Anonymous and loud,
I speak not for myself alone:
I represent the crowd.
We all of us are gentle folk,
And all opposed to violence:
Ensure that we remain that way,
Devote yourself to silence.

magine a town in the sixties —
A prairie town, battered by wind.

Strike Up The Banned

The Poet lives in a country where customs officers have sweeping powers to impound imported books, and withhold them from both stores and readers. Canada Customs, which is in effect a secret police force, has no public accountability, and operates with a mandate so broad they can abduct, with impunity, virtually any shipment of books, no matter how bland and innocuous its contents. Customs officers are notably fond of seizing books destined for gay and lesbian bookstores, such as Little Sister's in Vancouver and Glad Day in Toronto. That what is so clearly a vendetta can be so blatantly carried out by so powerful an agency against such small enterprises — and that nothing is done by the government that ostensibly regulates that agency to prevent such seizures, or at least to explain them — is astonishing. To say the very least. Here, The Poet cautions readers against the futility of trying to understand such actions. At the same time, he hopes they will lend their support to the booksellers whose livelihoods are threatened by such punitive actions, and to the larger cause of intellectual freedom. Thus endeth the rant.

Imagine a town in the sixties —
A prairie town, battered by wind.
Imagine a house in the town on the prairie
Where no one is known to have sinned.
Imagine a house in the town on the prairie, and let's call the year '64.
The wind, lack of sin and a house on the prairie:
Hands up if you've been here before.

Now, throw in a pre-adolescent —
A boy aged eleven or twelve.
The boy's pushing twelve and the house on the prairie's
Distinguished by burgeoning shelves.
The shelves are encumbered with numerous classics and morally
    uplifting texts:
Books like *The Robe*, and of course *Readers' Digest*,
Untroubled by rumblings of sex.

The boy on the prairie discovers
A secret cache kept by his dad
Of books of the kind that are sold in the drugstore
And generally known to be bad.
The covers show women with pendulous bosoms and skirts slit
    from ankle to hip:
Pendulous bosoms and dresses in tatters
And cigarettes dangling from lips.

The authors include Harold Robbins,
And Fanny Hill's found in the trove
He reads Henry Miller, *The Tropic of Cancer*,
And puts a new visage on love.
He joins the elite who have thumbed through *Lolita*, and also the
    Marquis de Sade,
Glancing from time to time over his shoulder,
Looking for Dad, or for God.

But neither one ever discovers —
At least not as far as he knows —
His secretive leafing through all that's forbidden
And hidden, verboten to show.
The books he's forbidden, the texts that are hidden, the words
    that are safely embalmed
Never awakened perversities latent,
And never brought hair to his palms.

The boy one day grew into manhood,
And all of the rights it accords —
The voting, the drinking, the sexual license,
The privileges and the rewards.
He grew into manhood, and laid manly plans: he would stride
    through the world primed and psyched!
Fearless of disapprobation and censure,
And reading whatever he liked!

But when he strode out, primed and eager
And tried to adhere to this creed,
He learned of the league of the uncivil servants
Who tell us what's fitting to read.
He learned of the nameless who censor the famous with never a
    whisper of why:
Faceless and nameless and hidden and blameless,
Empowered to seize and to lie.

He learned this news with some amazement.
He pondered it first, then he raged.
He stomped his foot loudly and shouted out proudly,
"Goddam it, I'm finally of age!
I'm finally of age, and no print on a page can corrupt me or lead
    me to sin."
He'd rave and he'd rant and he'd bluster and pant
And generally spit in the wind.

Now, let us decipher the moral:
It's time that we put this to rest.
We may as well own up, we're none of us grownups,
We none of us know what is best.
We none of us know what is best and the rest, then, is patently
    clear as a bell:
Our fears are all groundless, big Daddy has found us,
And Daddy — he treats us so well.

Envoi: To Critics Everywhere

Few people know as well as I just how very intellectually, morally, and physically taxing is the business of being self-appointed Poet Laureate. Mr. Richardson exhausts himself, and even imperils his mortal continuance, in the service of Art. I wrote this humble little offering myself one evening, while I was visiting The Bard. He lay prone on his chaise longue, dead to the world, drained by yet another day of committing random acts of beauty. Dark circles ringed his eyes. Every so often his limbs would twitch, and he would emit a sad little yelp. He was a pathetic sight, I can assure you. I felt my hackles rise, thinking how little he is understood, and how very much he has suffered at the hands of literary critics with insufficient wit, but great big axes to grind. This then, is not so much a cautionary tale, as a direct threat. Thank you for your kind attention.

Critics, when they read these poems,
Should neither wince nor cringe.
I know how to track you down,
And I have a syringe!

Laud and praise The Poet's work!
I pray you, take great pains!
I know how to track you down,
And I can find a vein!

Neither carp nor damn nor sneer
Throughout your close inspection.
I know how to track you down,
And I can give injections!

Venerate The Poet then,
And share my deep devotion.
I know how to track you down,
And I have lethal potions!

Here then are my closing words,
I now set down my pen:
I know how to track you down.
— Romana Clay, R.N.

BILL RICHARDSON

the self-appointed Poet Laureate of Canada, is a writer and broadcaster living in Vancouver, B.C. He is regular guest host of CBC Radio's *Gabereau* show, and his writing is featured regularly in the *Vancouver Sun*. He has written three previous books; *Canada Customs: Droll Recollections, Musings and Quibbles* (Brighouse Press) and *Queen of All the Dustballs and Other Epics of Everyday Life* (Polestar) were both nominated for the Stephen Leacock Medal for Humour, and in 1994, *Bachelor Brothers' Bed & Breakfast* (Douglas & McIntyre) was awarded the Stephen Leacock Medal.

CHUM McLEOD

is a freelance illustrator who lives and draws in Barrie, Ontario. Her artwork has been used for textbook illustration, magazines, children's books, and on book covers. She has illustrated *Aunt Fred Is A Witch* (Second Story Press), *Henry and the Cow Problem* (Annick), *There Will Always Be A Sky* (Nelson), *Come To Your Senses* (Annick), *The Snack Sneak* (Annick), and *White Horses and Shooting Stars: A Book of Wishes* (forthcoming, Polestar/Conari).